Who Is Love

Michele Prudlo

Presentation by *BookLeaf Publishing*

Web: www.bookleafpub.com

E-mail: info@bookleafpub.com

ISBN: 9789395756501

First edition 2022

DEDICATION

To my mother who has been there for me, not only through every single celebration and achievement, but most importantly loved me through all of my mistakes and faults. She always says, "I'll root for you in public every single day, but behind doors I will tell you as your friend, that was not the best choice you made."

Without her, I would not know what unconditional love is. I want to dedicate this book to her because it's the perfect book to show my appreciation. She lets me be me and still loves me regardless.

HDGDL!

ACKNOWLEDGEMENT

I would like to acknowledge and thank every person that I have loved and those who have loved me. A special thank you to those who continuously love me through hard times. I could not imagine this life without the love and affection humans and this universe gives.

PREFACE

I was inspired to write this book because I was questioning "Who Is Love". Is it a place, a memory, a smell, a person?

I believe Love looks, feels and sounds different to everyone. Every answer is different, but there is no wrong answer.

I've been in love many times. Every relationship, whether with others, myself, or the world, has been unique.

My purpose is to normalize Love as it shows up in different ways, good or bad, and how it develops each of us.

Remember that the pain doesn't fade, we just get used to living with it.

Grief Is Bigger Than Love

You can Love someone so much.
Show someone how much you Love them.
Every single day.
In so many different ways.

Grief on the other hand,
Is Love you can no longer express,show or give
to that special someone that is forever gone.

Transpire

When we were friends;
We laughed, played and trusted each other..

When we were lovers;
We smiled, loved and were passionate about
each other..

Now we are nothing;
We cry, miss and feel hurt.

We should be enemies;
So we can fight and hate each other until
eternity!

That One Place In The Universe

What is this beautiful place you are taking me to?
Where is this safe shelter you brought me to?
Why can only you take me to this secret address?

No one else has ever taken me to this magical location.

You said
We are here,
Home!

Tripped

I screamed "I AM DONE" as I walked out of the
door.
What I meant was..

Please hold me back.
Please run after me.
Please force me to come back.
Please make me work on us.
Please make me trip.

But instead you let me go.
I never looked back;
To see if you tripped running after me!

The Right Question

The question is not:
"Who will you choose as your forever,"

The real question is:
"Will you decide to choose with your head or
your heart?"

You Hate The Truth

You enjoy it when I lie.
You embrace it.
Reward me.
Absolutely love it.

When I tell you the truth you are mad.
You look away from me.
You hate it.
And therefore, I continue to lie.

The Narcissist

You are the Narcissist,
Now all of my dreams are dismissed.
You hold me back from life,
Have you been like this with your ex wife?

At the beginning you were so sweet,
Now you always think I cheat.
You won't let me go anywhere alone,
You get jealous and keep checking my phone.

Again you threw my phone against the wall and
it's broken,
I literally feel heartbroken.
You did not act like this when we started dating,
Now I see you and I am debating.

Will you hit me if I leave?
Or should I stay and be naive?
Which decision will make me feel relieved?
I think I'll start hiding money in my sleeve.

I am planning my escape,
For evidence I am taking the tape,
Everyone will know why I had to leave.
Leaving is what I will achieve.

I know you did not mean to be this way,
But the way you treated me was never okay.
I'm sorry I had to secretly pack my stuff and go,
I hope this tape is something I'll never have to show.

The One Before The One

I have loved you so deeply,
Kissed you so sweetly,
Held your hand tightly,
Protected your heart strongly,
Accepted your flaws freely.

Then I slipped away from you.
And now you're asking me for my
Love.
Kiss.
Hand.
Heart.
Me.

Now Numb-

I can't give that to you anymore.
My love is for someone else,
My kisses belong to him.
He holds my hand,
He protects my heart,
And accepts me for who I am.

Now Alive.

Would, Could, Should

Where would I be at right now If I
"shouldn't be there?"
Who would I love if I
"shouldn't love him?"
What would I do if I
"shouldn't do that?"
What would I wear If I
"shouldn't wear that"?
What would I say If I
"shouldn't say that?"
What would I see If I
"shouldn't see that?"
What would I feel If I
"shouldn't feel that?"
Where would I work if I
"shouldn't work there?"
Who would I spend my time with If I
"shouldn't spend time with them?"
What would I create If I
"shouldn't create that?"
How would I move my body If I
"shouldn't move it like that?"
What friends would I have If I
"shouldn't be friends with them?"

What and who would I be If I
"COULD" live my life without SHOULDN'T
anymore?
What If I stopped caring about outward
influences;
But instead make myself happy, then I
WOULD.

I would, could and should be right here where it
feels right.
I would, could and should feel so deeply with
you.
I would, could and should wear that dress.
I would, could and should say whatever I am
thinking.
I would, could and should feel the passion.
I would, could and should spend time with them.
I would, could and should dance like crazy.
I would, could and should be friends with her.
I would, could and should work the job I want.
I would, could and should create something
beautiful.
I would, could and should be my authentic self.

Fantasy Vs. Fairy Tale

I have this fantasy in my head.
So do you.
We imagine the improbable.

I want my fantasy of us to turn into a fairy tale.
So do you.
We imagine our future.

I want this future to turn into our afterlife.
So do you.
We are stuck in purgatory.

The One I Married

Before we met you went through a lot,
You haven't felt love like this before and forgot.
What did love feel like again?
Has she loved like this before with other men?
I fell in love with you because you treated me so well,
I loved when you said my name, Michele.
After being together for one year,
You said my dear,
Will you marry me?
You said you and I fit to a T.
I knew you were never romantic,
But I saw your heart was so gigantic.
So, I said yes,
After we got married all I caused you was stress.
I kept hurting you,
But you know I loved you too.
Where did the respect go?
Now, what do we have to show?
Where did the love go?
It's been so long ago.
Our love language is not the same,
But who is to blame?
Is this something that can be fixed?
My feelings for you are so mixed.

Can this ever be restored?
Or has this feeling too long been ignored?
You have always been there for me,
But these doubts are something I did not foresee.
You would do anything for me,
But who can I be?
Can I truly be me?
Every time I talk I get hurt,
I feel like you're asking me to convert.
Every time you speak,
You make me feel weak.
Weak like I can't accomplish anything,
I don't care anymore what others think.
But when did I lose my shine?
I am now trying to find it again in my glass of
wine.
You show me your love through action,
But where is the attraction?
You make me feel so ugly,
I certainly don't want to be snugly.
Where are the compliments,
I have to take supplements.
I am only getting older now,
Unhappiness is something I can no longer allow.
We said this would be forever,
However,
Maybe we're better not together.
Maybe you should hold somebody else's hand,

Maybe you'll be with someone who you can
better understand.
Someone that would be better for you,
Someone that appreciates everything you do.
Goodbye Lover,
I am sorry you had to discover,
My true cover.

Thank You

You were my first love ever.
I thought we would last forever!
I can not believe you just let me go,
I know this already happened 12 years ago.

The things you have taught and showed me,
I thought you would end up on one knee.
Instead you had no choice but to let me go,
And I know....

You wanted me to have a better life in a different
place,
In the past I never felt like I had to chase.
I know you were much older,
But I could always cry on your shoulder.

When the time came for me to move,
Even though I still disapprove,
I knew there was nothing I could do to prove it.
We had no choice but to split.

Thank you for letting me go;
I was able to grow.

Summer Love

You were so much fun,
I enjoyed our one- on- one.
During our summer break,
We spend every minute together by the lake.

Many nights we would enjoy a glass of
champagne,
You never had to explain.
You never had a complaint.

I know your love for me was real,
You didn't have to tell me how you feel.
You taught me self love,
You told me there was nothing about myself I
had to get rid of.

You told me how beautiful I was every day,
I was so upset when I had to go away.
Since I was gone,
Out of sight out of mind; withdrawn.

I'm sorry I never got a hold of you again,
Hung out instead in Germany with Ken.
I never thought you were that serious about us,
We never really took the time to discuss.

I went back home and didn't call,
Discussing us being exclusive; I don't recall.
Few months later you send me a gift in the mail,
I did not even bother to send you a thank you
E-mail.

I feel bad on how I treated you,
I hope you know I'll always care about you too.

Kevin

You treated me the very best,
I would trust you so much and lay on your chest.
You would save me during every panic attack,
You'd calm me down and make me relax.

You wrote this beautiful sonnet,
Describing me as a powerful woman.
You saw me as suitable.
But I told you something inexcusable.

I told you we can not date,
You were just a little too late.

I told you I wasn't over an ex,
So we decided to keep it with having sex.
I figured you'd fall in love with me,
But it can't be us three.

You'd always hold my hand,
I used you and you'd always understand.
You'd always bring me home safely,
I appreciated you greatly!

Daily!

Tears Are Not Wet

You and I share the same soul.
I am now only half of me;
Will this pain go away?
I cry and see my reflection in the mirror.
I see the tears,
Wipe them away but,
they are not wet.
The tears are deeper than that..
I see them on the surface of my skin.
But the tears are in my heart,
My broken heart feels the agony
Of never speaking to you again.

Soulmate

We used to be very good friends,
Things took a huge turn and we had to make
amends.
We tried to make it right but it was too late,
At that moment we knew we could never date.
I still remember how you used to call me a gem,
And you know my first fish's name used to be
Chem.
You always held the door for me,
We planned on running away to Tennessee.
You said you'd give up all of your plans you
had,
Being with me you'd never again have to feel
sad.
You said you'd hold our ring when you feel
stressed,
You would no longer feel depressed.
Around me you would never,ever, have to fake
who you truly are,
I could see every single scar.
We used to think the exact same way,
Together we felt beyond just okay.
You always asked me how I am feeling,

Though you're the one that was working on
healing.
No matter what time or day, you'd meet me at
our spot,
No matter how difficult it got.
I am sure for you it became a lot,
Having to worry about getting caught.
We would sit there and talk about anything at all,
When we didn't see each other I always knew I
could call.
We have no picture together at all,
I was too busy to fall.
You felt everything I felt,
We would constantly make each other's heart
melt.
You meant everything to me in my life,
Though I was somebody else's wife.
We talked about having a child of our own,
Now we are blocked on each other's phone.
I would never let anyone call me babe ever,
I let you because I thought we would last
forever.
You made sure to tell me I will forever be
enough,
I knew you meant that even when moments got
tough.
You asked if I'll watch anything with you in the
evening,

We agreed it would be something from Stephen King.
You would tell me to go through the orange light,
Now we are both hurt and we can not reunite.
I am the fuel and you are the fire,
We did anything to fulfill our desire.
The way you looked at me I knew you loved me so much,
The future is something we can no longer see or touch.
"In another life we'll be together" is what you texted me,
You made it sound like a guarantee.
In this life we were only able to live this short fantasy,

———-----

We wanted to live this fairy tale,
Now we walk through this earth separated and pale.
You said "everything will be okay my cookie",
But I can't smell your scent anymore on my hoodie.
Every car that passes by I think this might be you,
Wondering if you are with someone new.
Only you and I know what we had,
Though every single person around us is now mad.

My family thinks what made me to this was
drugs,
All I wanted was your special never ending
hugs.
Maybe tomorrow you'll be mad at me and want
to throw a brick through my window,
I guess we are both confused about me leaving
and are going through a limbo.
When we got caught,
I was ready to be shot.
In this case I wouldn't have to feel this current
pain,
This love is something I can not explain.
Get your shit together,
So you can get better.
But still at night I stare at the stars and think,
Maybe you also see me when you blink.
I remember the time I looked into your eyes and
saw your soul,
Now I live day by day with this hole.
I remember when you turned down the music for
me to talk,
All I see you do now is you walk.
Walk away from me,
Wondering if there will ever be a "we"?
I keep imagining this fantasy of you and I,
Do I really have to text you bye?
Life with you was just like a movie,
You were truly everything to me.

I believe I'll forever remain special to you,
Even when others tell me you're with someone new.
Regardless if that is the truth.
We will never again sit across a booth.
We can no longer play footsies
I wish I could seize..
The moment
The love
The kiss
The hug
The talk
The dream
The fairy tale
The YOU
All of you.

Paradoxical

You look into my eyes,
And yet you still see everything pure.

I promise I am NOT the prettiest,
The funniest,
The purest,
The most loyal,
The best behaved,
The smartest,
The most talented.

But yet you still see me the best way possible
like I am all of those things.

You look into my eyes,
And yet you still see everything alluring.

All the feelings I can make you feel.
All the love I can give you to feel loved.
All the words I can say to reassure you.
All the things I'll do to make you feel safe and
protected.
All the work I put into making this work.
All the hate I'll have for people that don't love
you.

All the love I have for people that love you.
All the patience I'll have for you to feel calm.
You think I can give you the world.

But can I?
Will you leave me If I can't?
Will you break my heart?

You look into my eyes again,
And you see everything that seems impossible;
Everything that seems imaginable and
paradoxical.

You believe I can reach the stars.
You believe I can catch fish in the lake with my
bare hands.
You believe I can become famous and stay
humble.
You believe I can walk around the world without
being exhausted.
You believe I can drink fire and eat water.
You believe I can think upside down and in
reverse.

You look into my eyes one last time,
You tell me you see LOVE when you see me.
You said you don't know if we can anchor the
world together,
GOOD

Bye.

Roses Are Not Always Red

All these songs used to be a melody,
After meeting you they all now make sense.
The happy and the sad ones..

Every cuisine used to taste good,
After meeting you they taste so much better.
When I can eat..

Flowers used to be pretty,
After meeting you they seem so much more
vibrant.
Even the poisonous ones..

Strangers used to be nice,
After meeting you I love everyone.
Even the sinners..

My house used to keep me safe,
After meeting you it seems free from danger,
Even when the fire broke out in my kitchen..

My love to God used to be there,
After meeting you I can't possibly love God
more because he sent me your way.
Even after you left me..

Roses used to be just red,
After meeting you, you showed me the rainbow
colored ones.
Even the dead ones.

Who Is To Blame

Who is to blame when the words of affirmations
are gone;
Who is to blame when the acts of services are
gone;
Who is to blame when the quality time is gone;
Who is the blame when the physical touch is
gone;
Who is to blame when the receiving gifts are
done;
Did I lose my value because it is all gone?

Love,
You don't have to know who is to blame.
Make yourself a cup of coffee in the morning,
Go for a drive and stop to absorb the beautiful
view,
Lay in bed and feel yourself,
Buy yourself that shirt you kept passing by.

Love,
You never lost your value.
They lost their vision to see what you
Wanted.
Desired.
Deserved.

Your value has never left.
For whatever reason;
Their view of you has
just
changed.

You are not to blame.

Myself

I smoke a lot of cigarettes,
And I make plenty of empty threats.
Sometimes I sleep a lot,
And I don't consider myself hot.

I truly love so deeply,
But I only wash my hair twice weekly.
I definitely cry a lot at night,
And I get too passionate when I fight.

I hurt people all the time,
But I love you regardless if you committed a
crime.
I have never been called smart,
But I do have a pure heart.

My soul is so pure,
But sometimes I am immature.
I have given love to many boyfriends,
But seem to never keep new friends.

I always seem to screw things up every day,
But I never care what other people say.
You can call me a bitch and I don't care,
That's why I am so limited with what I share.

There are only a few people I trust,
I know there are people that look at me with
disgust.
I love to be alone.
And my favorite scent is men's cologne.

I love birds and cats,
And I only kind of know how to change flats.
I love to take baths alone,
And I don't like anyone going through my
phone.

I am not patient at all,
Sometimes I will build a wall.
I have no idea how to dance.
And I need to know every appointment in
advance.

I can't understand how people enjoy to work
out,
And I never know my route.
I repeatedly listen to my favorite song,
And sometimes I am wrong.

Many moments I am blonde,
When we fight I might decide not to respond.
I sing under the shower,
At my funeral I don't want a single flower.

Sometimes I clean too much,
And my love language is physical touch.
I believe every person consists of red flags,
And we still love when the S/O nags.

Every single person on this earth has a soulmate
out there,
The right one will love you regardless and show
you that they truly care.
Make sure you love yourself with your flaws,
Love, it has no laws.

Who Is Love

Who is love?
What is love?
Where is love?
What does it feel like?
What does it look like?
What does it smell like?
What does it sound like?

Is love a person?
Is it a feeling?
Is it a place?
Is it myself?
Is it a taste?
Is it a scent?
Is it a choice?

We keep asking ourselves these questions.
We know the answer but we keep trying to avoid
it.
You know what and who love is.

Its not their scent,
Its not their smile,
Its not their words,
Its not their wealth

Its not their success,
Its not their actions,
Its not their gender, age or race,
Its not their family,
Its not their taste,

Love is the one who you feel at home with.
Love is the one that makes you feel safe.
Love is the one you want to be with on the good
and bad days.
Love is the one that you could never imagine
hurting.
Love is the one you can not see yourself living
without.
Love is the one you would die for.

I was once told love is a choice,
But if there is no love present, how can you
make that choice to love?
Make a choice to feel at home with them?
Make the choice to feel safe with them?
Make the choice you can't live without them?
It sounds like forced love and not true love.
YOU KNOW who love is and who is not.

Who Is Love?

Love is Them.

The one you thought about while you were
reading this.

www.ingramcontent.com/pod-product-compliance
Lightning Source LLC
LaVergne TN
LVHW021314200726
843509LV00012B/1908